NAPA VALLEY

GERALD & MARC HOBERMAN

NAPA VALLEY

GERALD & MARC HOBERMAN

Photographs celebrating the pride of America's wine country

Text by Jan Austerman & Rebecca Yerger

UNA PRESS, INC.
in association with
THE GERALD & MARC HOBERMAN COLLECTION
CAPE TOWN • LONDON • NEW YORK

Concept, design, and production control: Gerald & Marc Hoberman
Photography: Gerald & Marc Hoberman *Reproduction:* Marc Hoberman
Text: Jan Austerman, Rebecca Yerger *Editor*: Roelien Theron
Layout: Christian Jaggers
Cartography: Peter Slingsby

Mighty Marvelous Little Books are published by
The Gerald & Marc Hoberman Collection
PO Box 60044, Victoria Junction, 8005, Cape Town, South Africa
Telephone: 27-21-419 6657 Fax: 27-21-418 5987 e-mail: office@hobermancollection.com
www.hobermancollection.com

International marketing, corporate sales, and picture library

United Kingdom, Republic of Ireland, Europe
Marc Hoberman
Hoberman Collection (UK)
250 Kings Road, London, SW3 5UE
Telephone: 0207 352 1315 Fax: 0207 352 4617
e-mail: uk@hobermancollection.com

United States of America, Canada, Asia
Laurence R. Bard
Hoberman Collection (USA), Inc. / Una Press, Inc.
PO Box 880206, Boca Raton, FL 33488, USA
Telephone: (561) 542 1141
e-mail: hobcolus@bellsouth.net

ISBN 0-972982-27-2

First published 2005, Reprinted 2006

Printed in Singapore

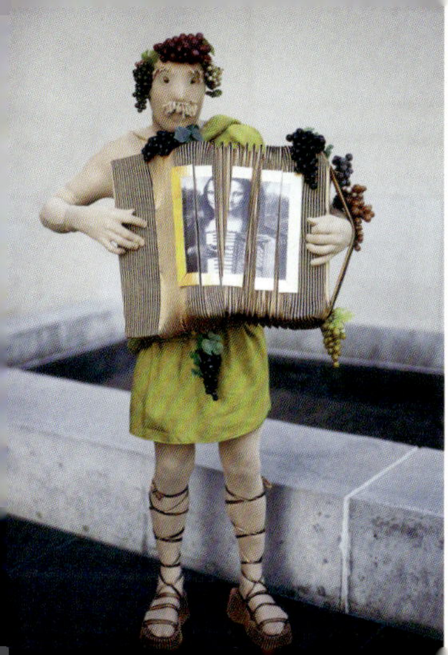

CONTENTS

FOREWORD

Napa—the land of plenty—was the name bestowed by the Wappo Indian tribe who inhabited the valley hundreds of years before the arrival of the Spaniards and gold rush settlers. Wildlife, salmon, waterfowl, and fruit trees endured long before acres of vineyards spread across the valley. Today it is still a land of plenty to the thousands fortunate to live here and the millions more who come annually to delight in the wines, food, hospitality, and breathtaking beauty.

Gerald and Marc Hoberman have brilliantly captured the magic and spirit of the Napa Valley through their stunning and vivid photographs. Your astonishment will be like that of a first-time tourist. For those privileged to have visited the valley before or for those who live here, the Hobermans' Napa Valley will fascinate readers by revealing new people, places, and perspectives.

It is easy to be enraptured by the bounty of the Napa Valley when you witness the Hobermans' spectacular sights of spiraling geysers, voluminous balloon rides, perfectly manicured vineyards, and awe-inspiring mountain vistas. Devoted winemakers, growers, chefs, restaurateurs, inn keepers, and even the every-day Napa eccentrics are brought to life in stellar images. Behind-the-scenes photographs reveal what many believe to be the heart and soul of Napa—a

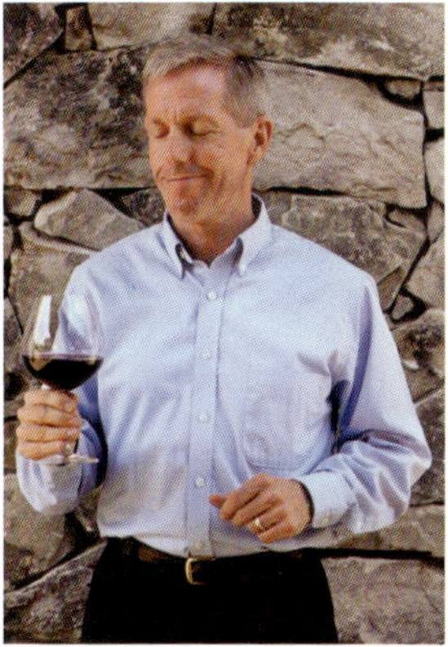

philanthropic valley willing to support charitable causes, everything from farm worker housing to health and family services to new cultural landscapes.

Napa is the land of plenty, but also a dynamic, evolving valley and with that comes challenges. Growth versus non-growth, environmental concerns, affordable housing, and adequate transportation—issues that face many communities in the world today. Yet Napa is truly unique and its inhabitants, businesses, and visitors alike genuinely cherish this sacred land and are devoted to preserving what Mother Nature provided.

Thankfully, the Hobermans' gift of amazing images and discerning knowledge of the Napa Valley will endure forever. Linger over the scenes while sipping a glass of Napa Valley Cabernet and you will be swiftly whisked away to an exquisite place with plenty to savor and treasure.

Peter Marks

Peter Marks
Master of Wine, Napa Valley

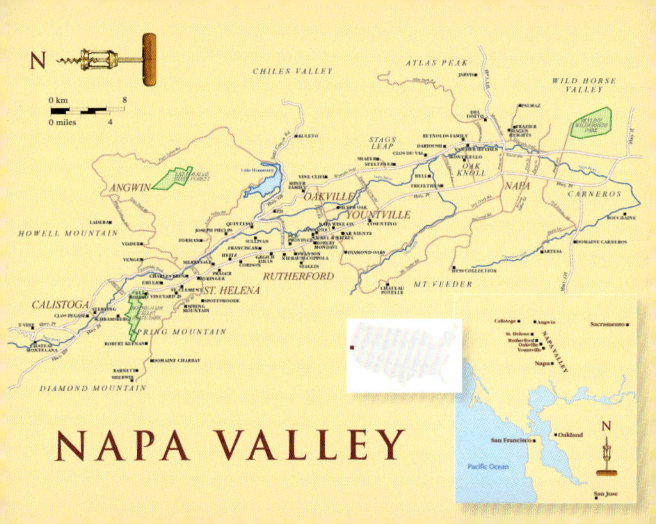
NAPA VALLEY
N
0 km
8
0 miles
4
CHILES VALLEY
ATLAS PEAK
WILD HORSE VALLEY
STAGS LEAP
OAK KNOLL
NAPA
CARNEROS
ANGWIN
OAKVILLE
YOUNTVILLE
HOWELL MOUNTAIN
RUTHERFORD
ST. HELENA
MT. VEEDER
CALISTOGA
SPRING MOUNTAIN
DIAMOND MOUNTAIN
Calistoga
Angwin
Sacramento
St. Helena
Rutherford
Oakville
Yountville
NAPA VALLEY
Napa
San Francisco
Oakland
Pacific Ocean
San Jose
N

INTRODUCTION

Our discovery of the Napa Valley was a delightful consequence of a visit to this famed wine region to showcase it in our book *San Francisco*. We were privileged to have met so many wonderful people in the Napa Valley, including some who have become world-renowned legends in their own time. Their foresight, expertise, and vision have ensured the continuity and preservation of the valley's beauty and charm.

We were struck by the natural beauty of the valley, the obvious sophistication and precision of its viticulture, and the premium, award-winning wines that are produced there. The valley's fascinating terroirs and microclimates, huge investments, pride of product, and prestige are the hallmarks of Napa Valley wines—a stark contrast to the dark days of Prohibition.

This region is renowned for its gourmet restaurants including arguably the finest restaurant in the world! The choice and standards of accommodation naturally match the only criterion of the valley—excellence!

Through the photographs in this book, some taken from helicopters and hot-air balloons, we wish to share with you the special attributes and wonders of the Napa Valley from our perspective. A mere stone's throw from the charms of San Francisco, the high-tech Silicon Valley, and the world-class Stanford and Berkeley universities, the Napa Valley is a gem of viticulture, fine dining, and elegant rural life.

Gerald Hoberman

GERALD HOBERMAN
Napa Valley

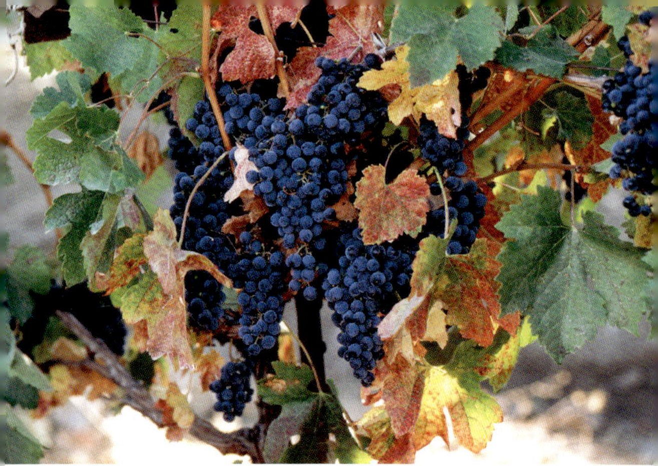

12 “In wine there is truth.” Pliny the Elder, *Natural History* (1st c.).

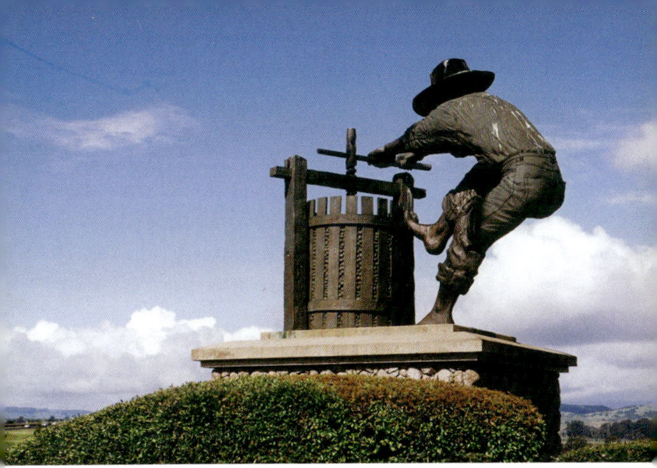

The Grape Crusher, by Gino Miles, is a Napa Valley landmark.

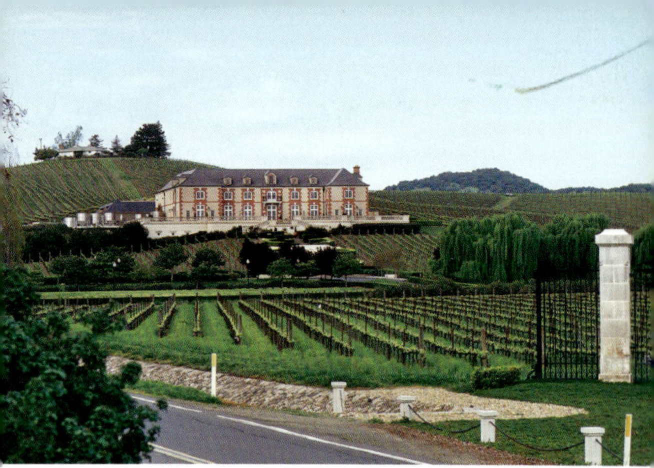

14 Classic sparkling wine is produced at Domaine Carneros.

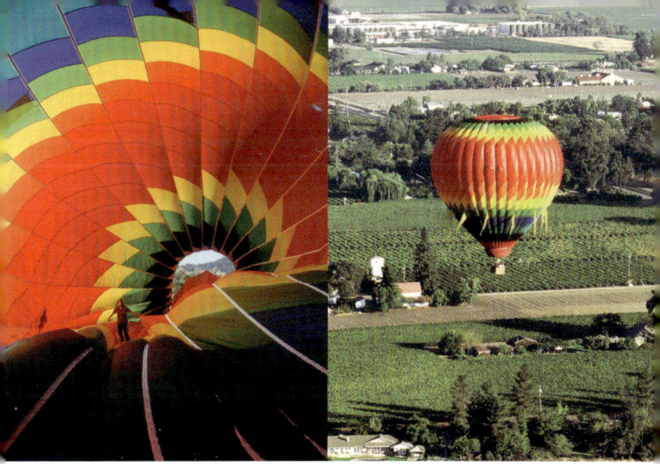

Hot-air ballooning takes visitors high above Napa Valley's vineyards.

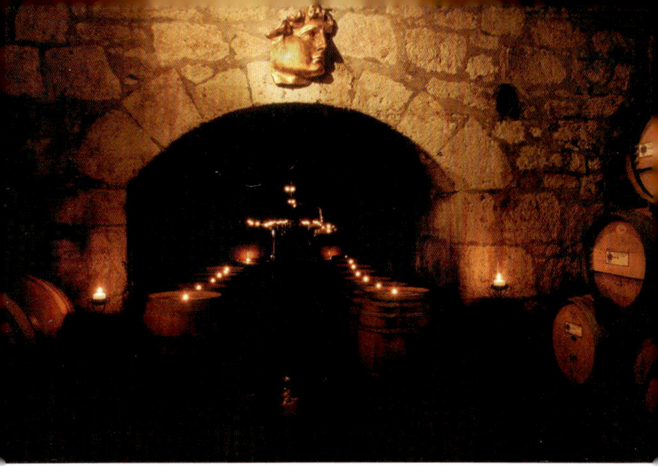

16 The winery and caves at Del Dotto date back to 1885.

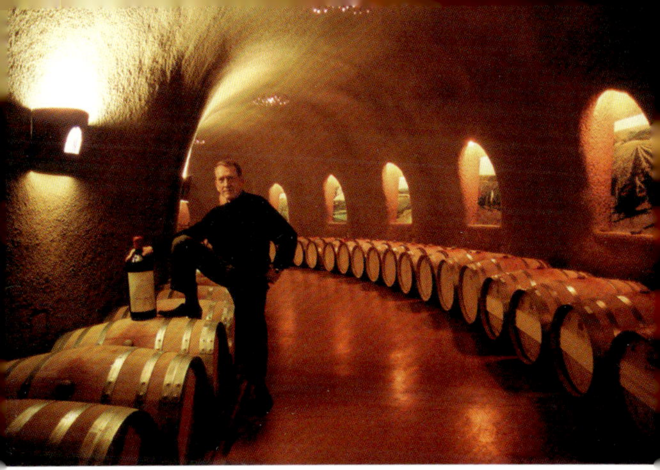

Jarvis Winery is housed within the eastern hills of northern Napa.

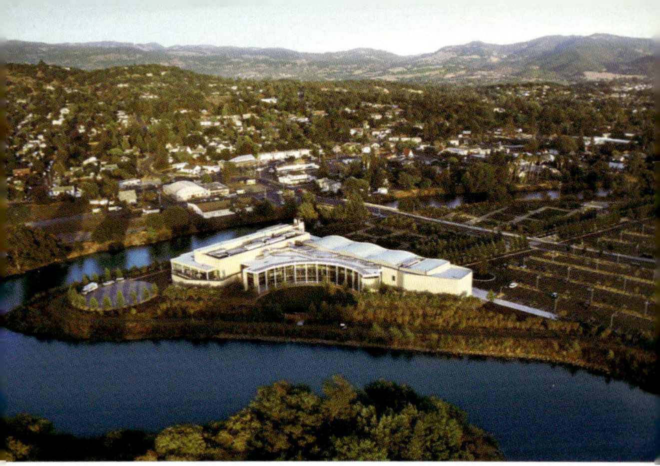

18 Copia: The American Center for Wine, Food, and the Arts.

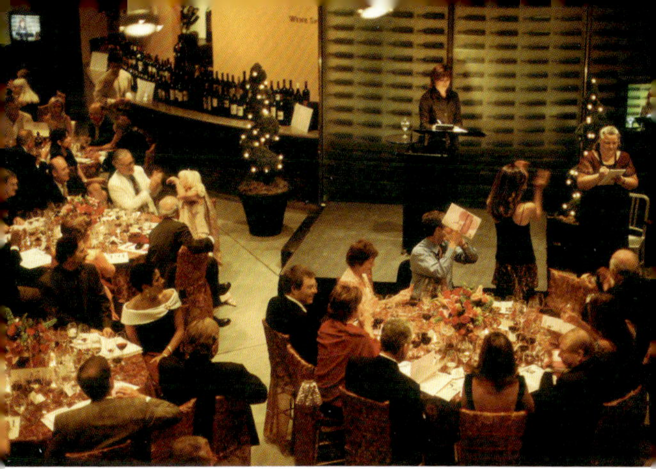

The Bacchus Gala and Auction honors Copia's Wine Award winners.

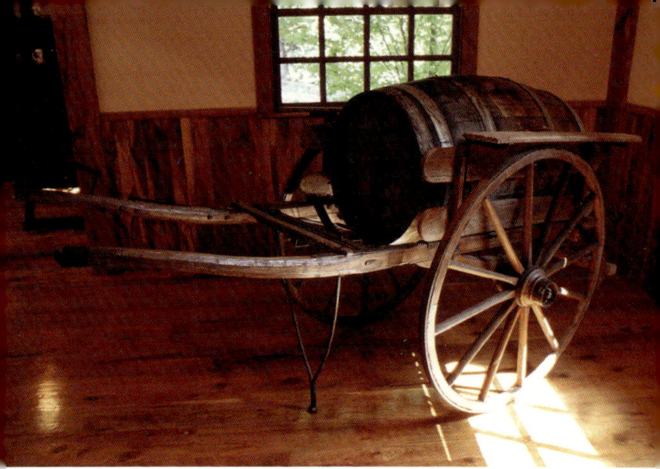

 Palmaz Winery has the largest wine caves in the Napa Valley.

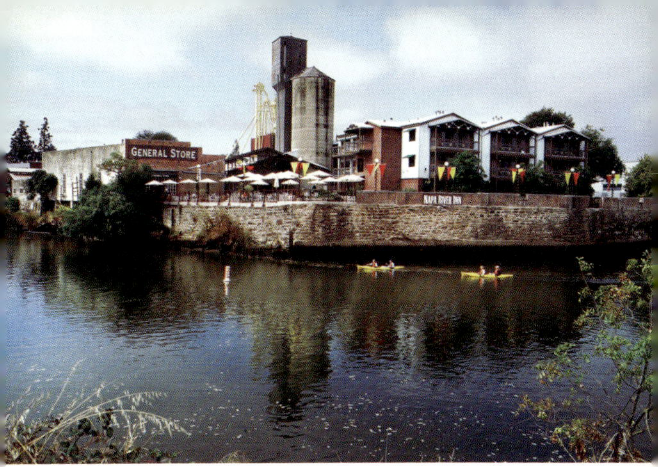

Napa River Inn is part of the historic Hatt-Napa Mill Complex.

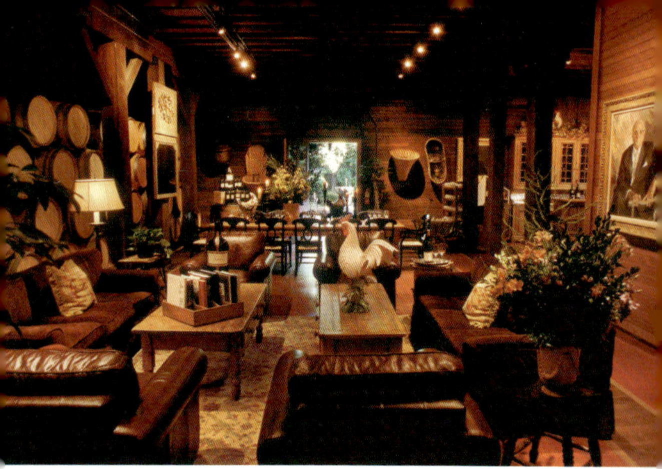

22 The 600-acre Trefethen Vineyards estate is in the Oak Knoll district.

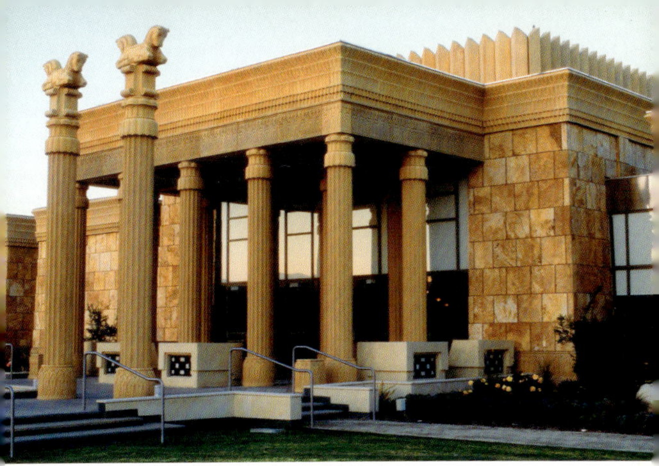

Darioush winery's distinctive design draws on Persian Classicism.

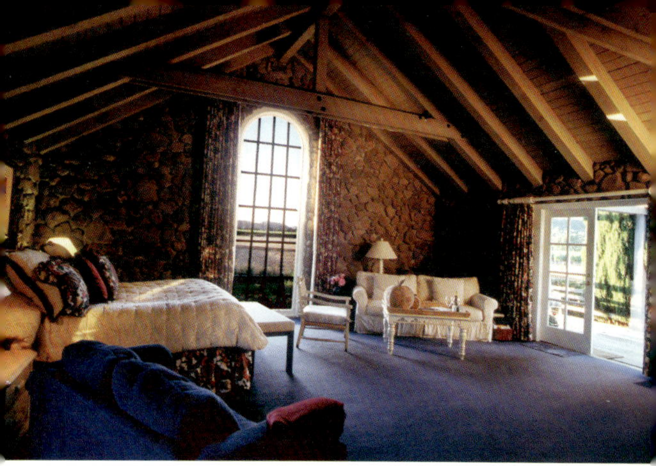

24 Oak Knoll Inn provides superb luxury, serenity, and seclusion, with

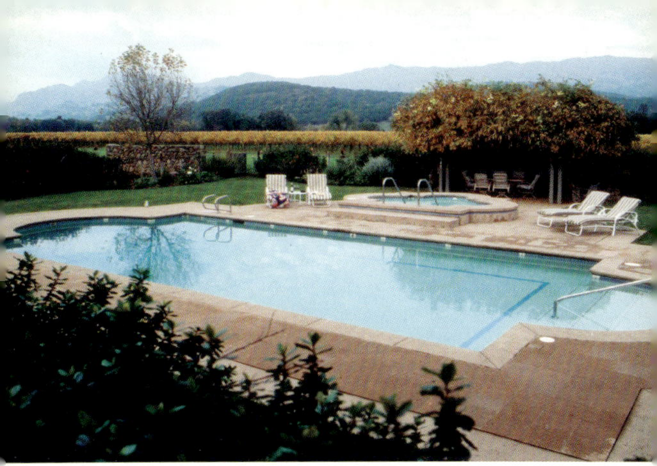

magnificent panoramic views of vineyards and mountains.

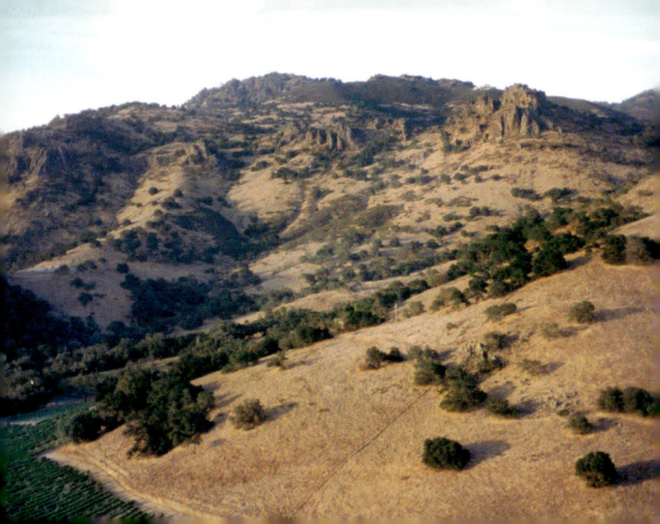

Left A Native American legend tells of a mystical stag in the eastern hills of Napa Valley which could be seen leaping from crag to crag on full-moon nights. Over time, these palisades became known as Stags Leap.

Right Dedicated wine aficionado, Kari Auringer is a member of the home wine-makers' support group, the Napa Valley Home Wine-makers Association (NVHWA), established in 1972.

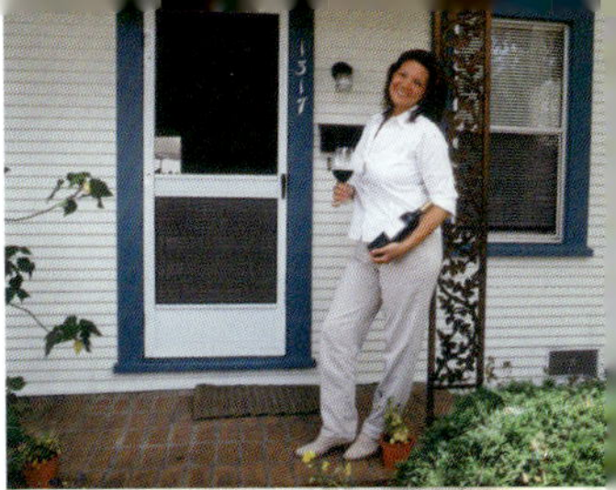

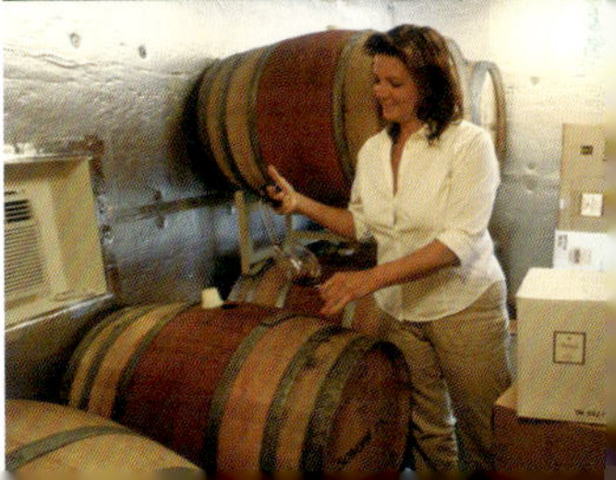

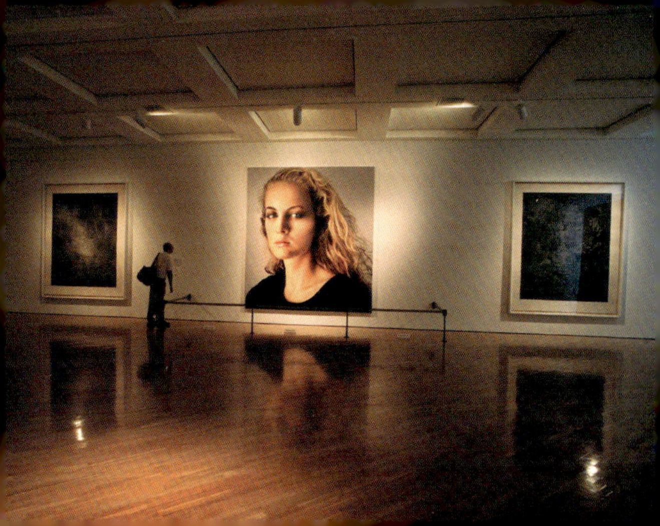

Left The 13,000-square-foot art gallery at the Hess Collection Winery features an international collection of art works, such as *Johanna II* by Franz Gertsch.

Right Jan Smits, a native of Holland, and his flag-festooned bicycle are a familiar sight on the roads of Napa Valley.

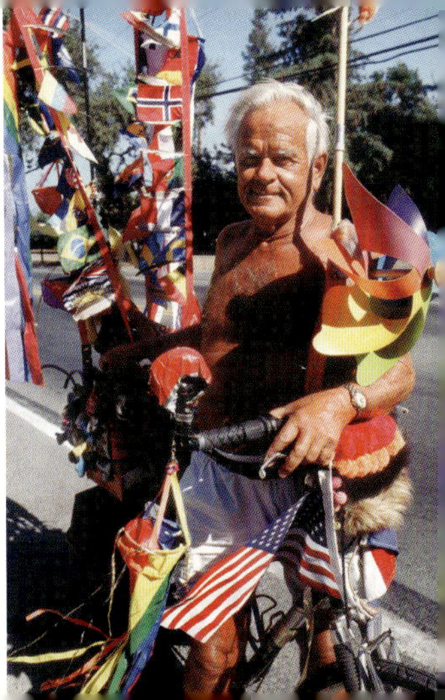

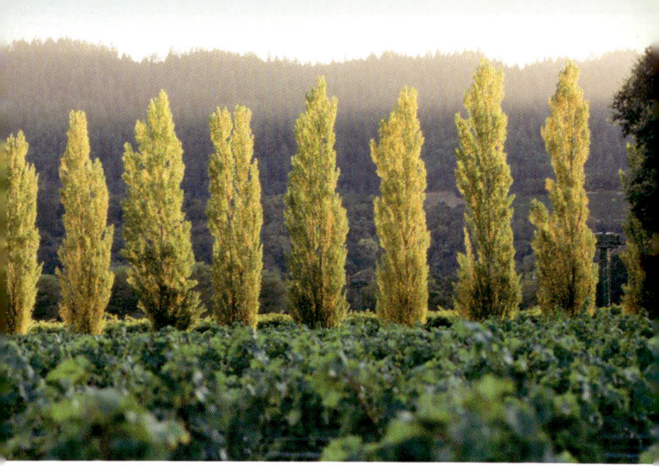

30 Trees stand sentinel at sunset.

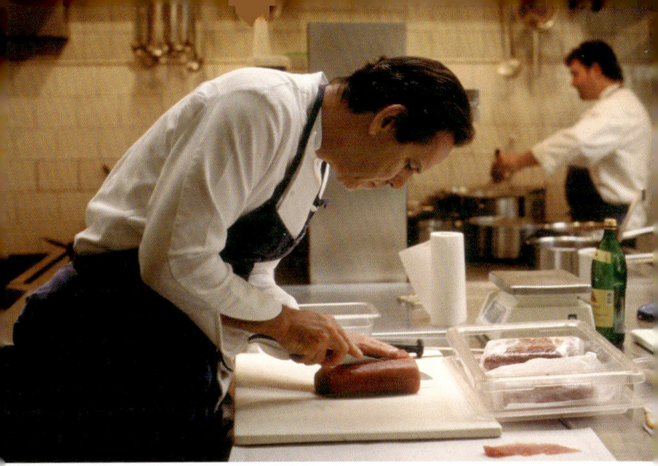

The French Laundry is one of the most famous restaurants in the world.

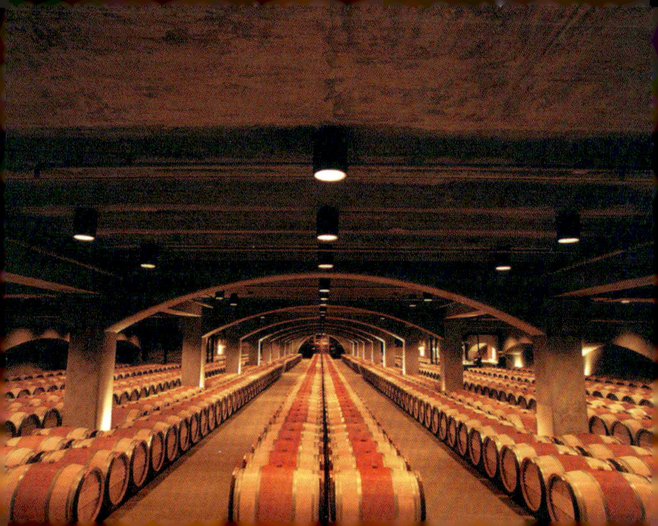

Left At Robert Mondavi Winery premium red wine is aged in oak barrels to bring out the subtle aromas and expansive natural flavors inherent in the grapes.

Right A state-of-the-art facility, Opus One Winery represents a joint venture between two preeminent wine families, Mondavi and Rothschild, resulting in distinctive wines that draw on the best winemaking traditions from both Bordeaux and California.

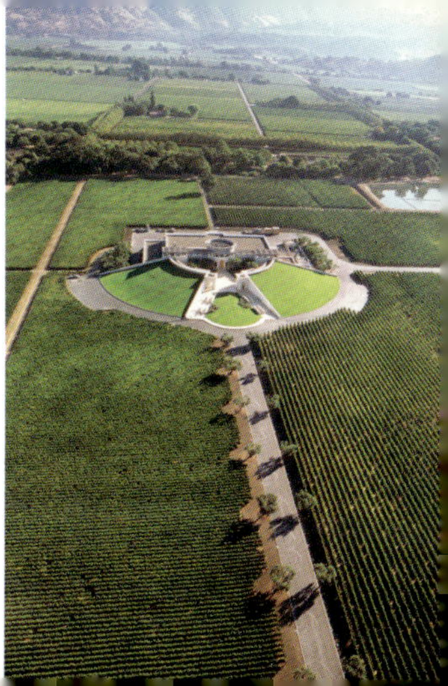

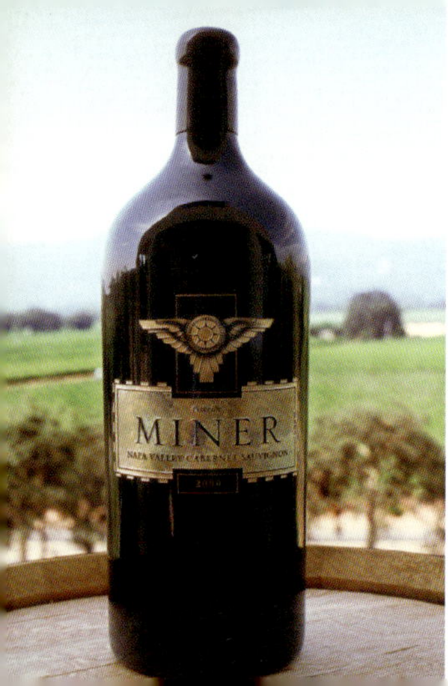

Left Miner Family Vineyards is situated along the eastern hills of the Oakville appellation, Napa Valley. Its unique wine label is based on an ancient Assyrian relief depicting the winged sun god.

Right The Niebaum-Coppola Estate Winery, owned by film-maker Francis Ford Coppola, was initially known as Inglenook Winery. The Rutherford winery was established by Captain Gustave Niebaum, a wealthy fur trader, between 1883 and 1887.

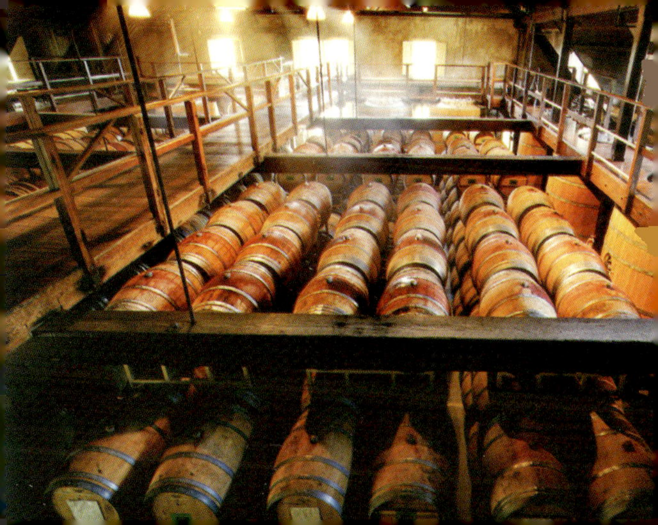

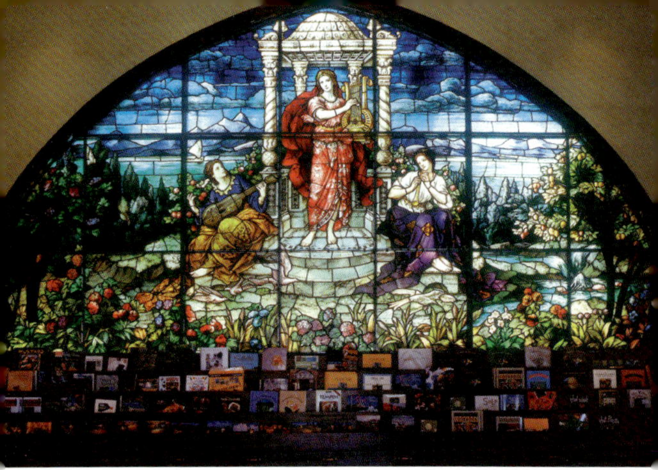

36 A 1906 glass window adorns the tasting room at Peju Province Winery.

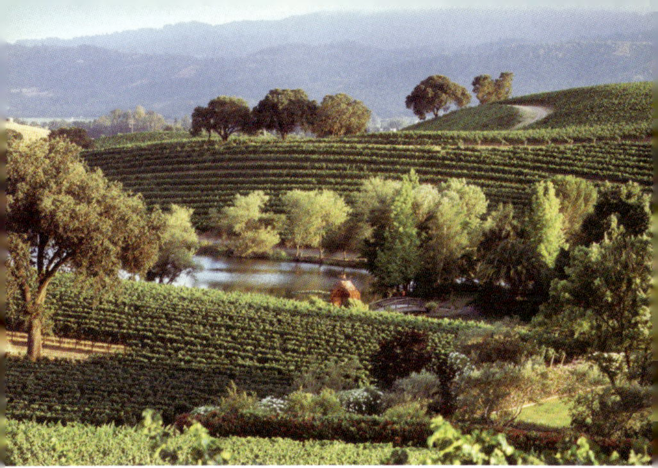

The 280-acre Quintessa is situated in the Rutherford appellation.

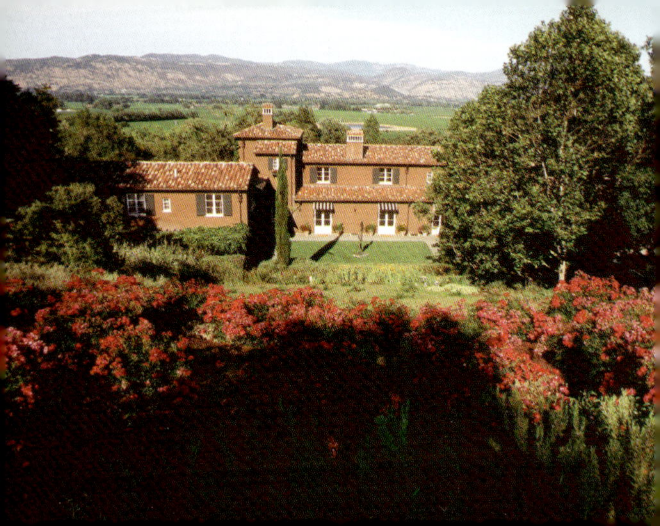

Left Garen and Shari Staglin established Staglin Family Vineyard in 1985. Its 24,000-square-foot underground winery was completed in 2002. The winery produces Cabernet Sauvignon, Chardonnay, and Sangiovese.

Right While long ago grape stomping was the only way to crush fruit, today it forms part of celebratory events such as the annual Grape Stomp held at Franciscan Estates.

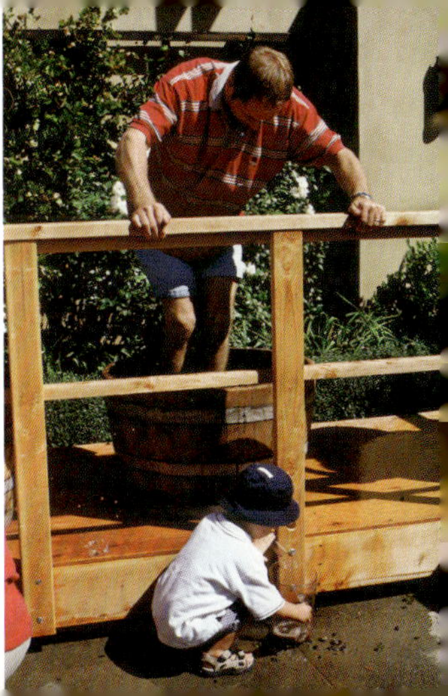

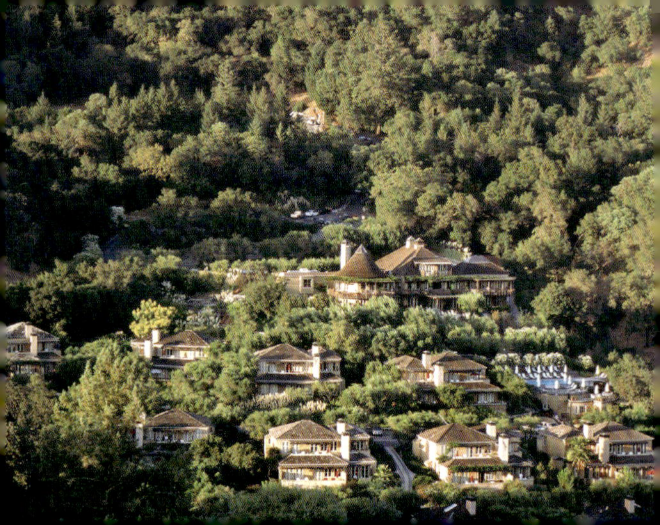

Left The cottages and suites at the magnificent Auberge du Soleil resort are perched on a hillside above Napa Valley in Rutherford.

Right Croatian immigrant Miljenko "Mike" Grgich, is an icon of the Napa Valley. This renowned winemaker runs Grgich Hills Winery together with his daughter, Violet, and grand-nephew, Ivo Jeramaz.

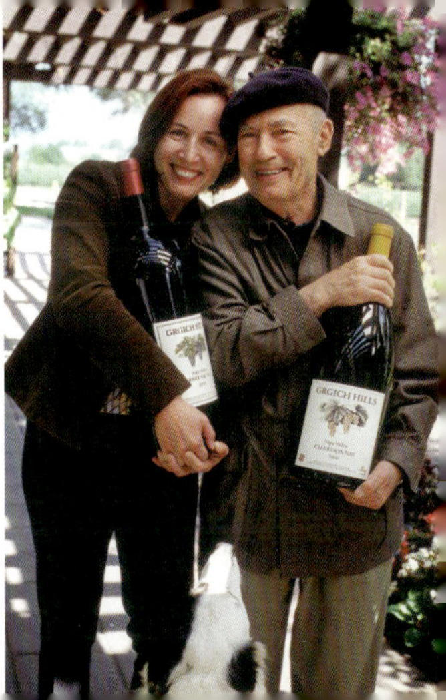

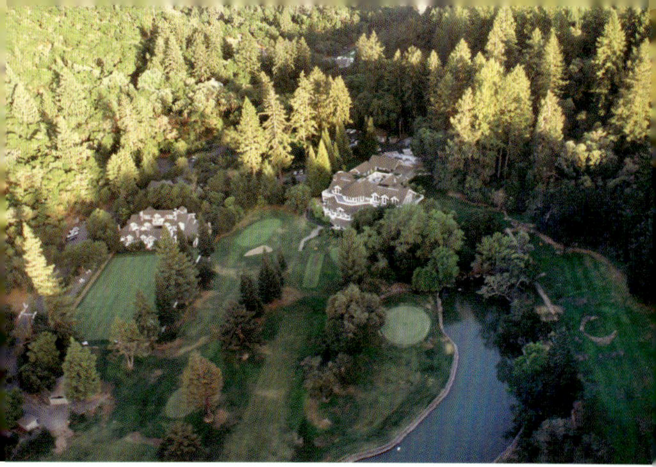

 Surrounded by 250 acres of tranquil woodlands and shrub-covered

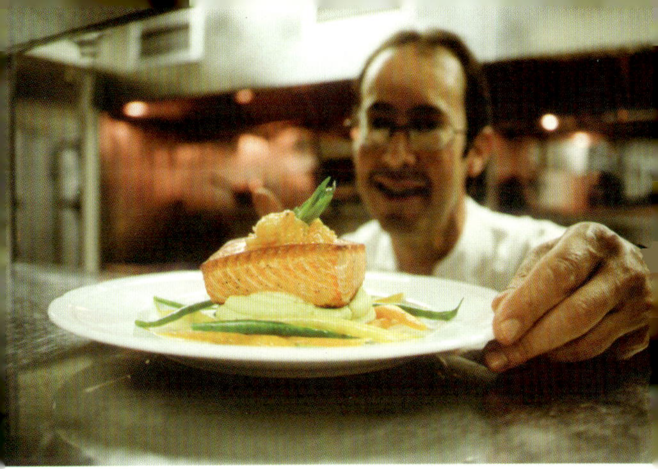

hills, Meadowood Napa Valley resort is located near St. Helena.

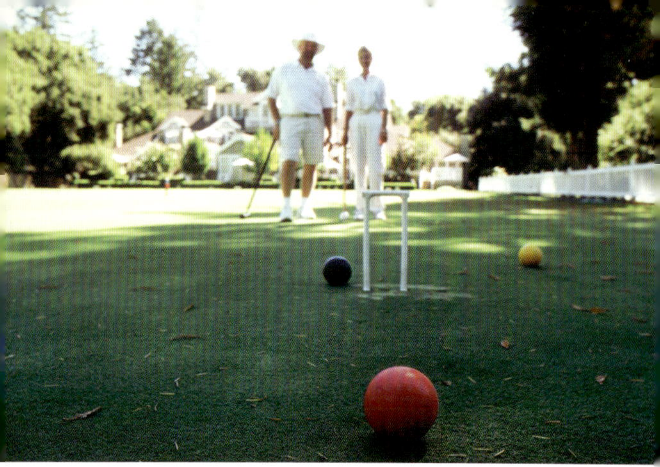

44 Meadowood is home to the annual Croquet Classic.

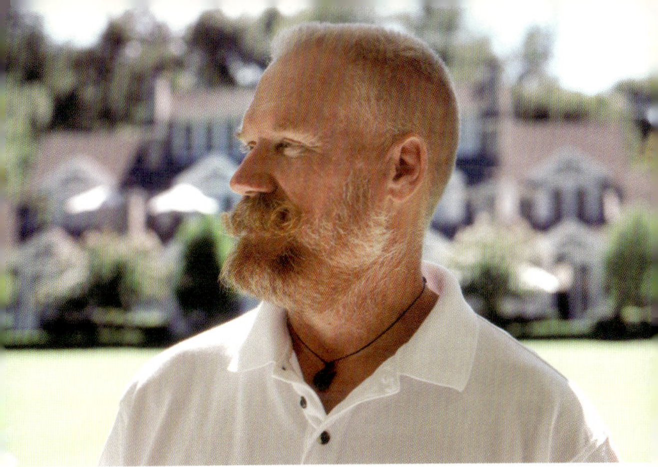

Legendary croquet player, Jerry Stark is the resident pro.

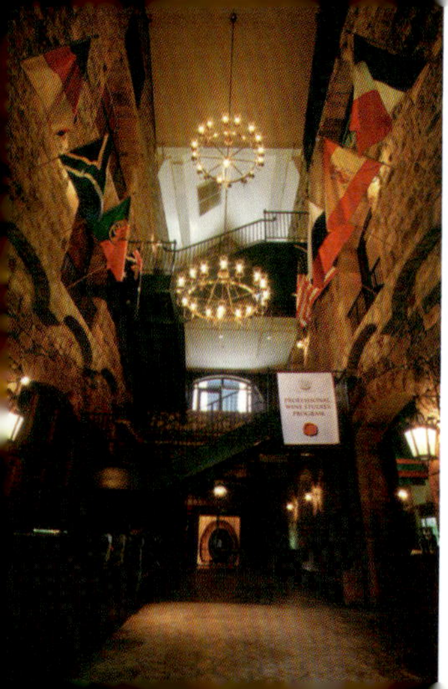

Left The Culinary Institute of America (CIA) was founded in Hyde Park, New York in 1946. In 1995 it established its West Coast campus in the Napa Valley.

Right Located along Main Street in St. Helena, Taylor's Refresher opened in 1949. While the original, classic, drive-in façade that characterised old style American roadside cafés has been retained, a few changes have since been made to the interior, including the addition of a wine bar.

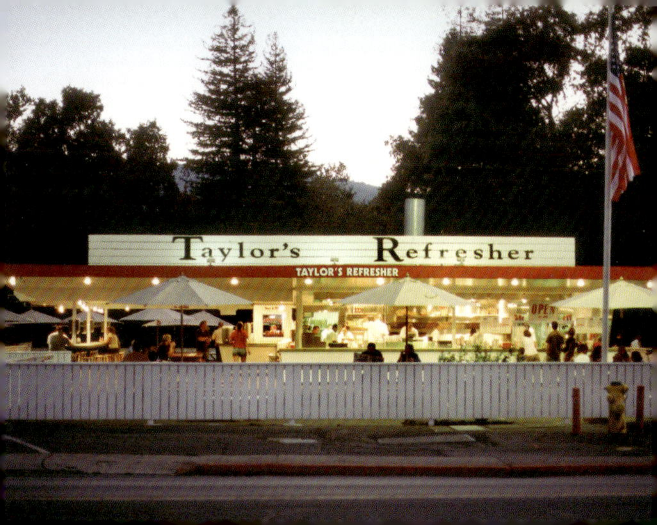
Taylor's Refresher
TAYLOR'S REFRESHER
OPEN

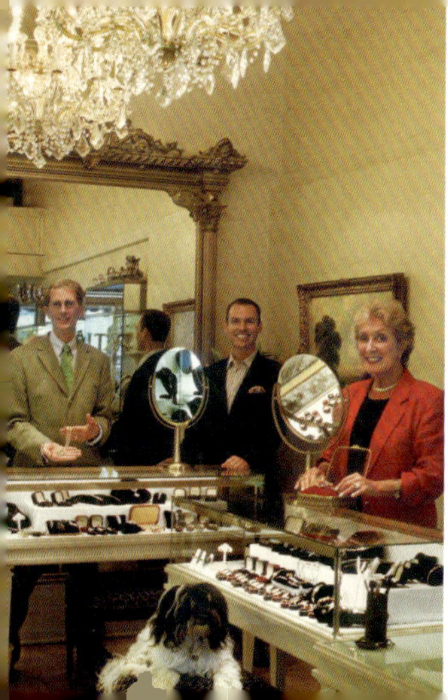

Left Inspired by a shared passion for beautiful jewelry, Marcus Robbins and Wayne Armstrong opened Patina, a fine estate and period jewelry shop, in St. Helena in 1995.

Right Jeff Yates is the proprietor of St. Helena Wine Merchants, located between Rutherford and St. Helena. The family-owned business opened its doors to the public in 1983, and specializes in procuring rare and hard-to-find wines.

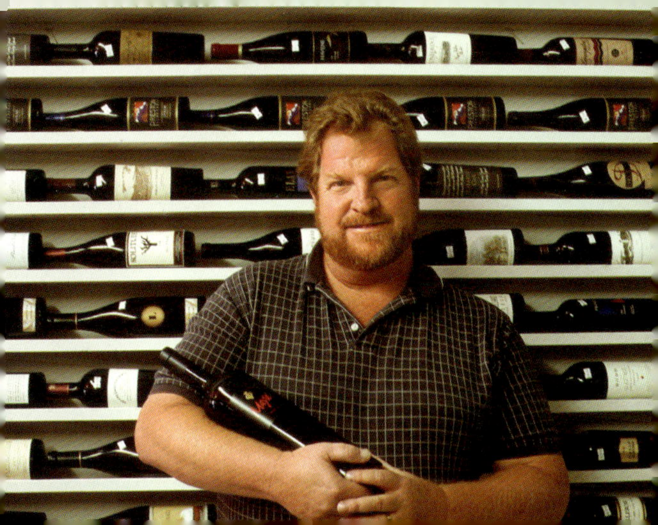

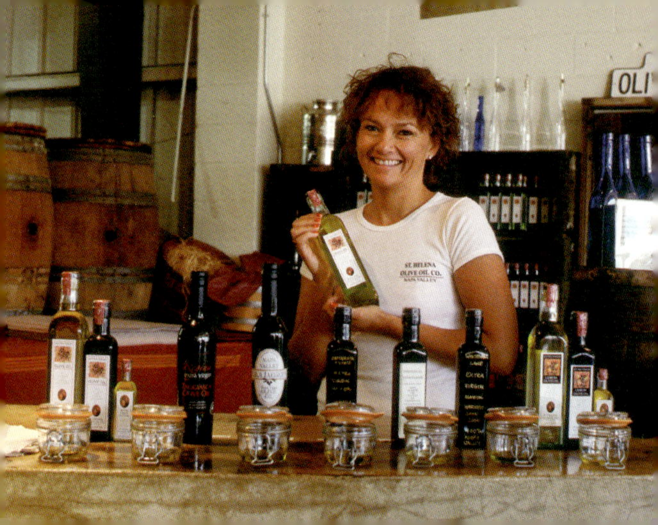
OLI
ST. HELENA
OLIVE OIL CO.
NAPA VALLEY

Left Founded by Peggy O'Kelly, the St. Helena Olive Oil Company was one of the first businesses in the Napa Valley to be devoted to the production of olive oil.

Right Situated east of St. Helena, Heitz Cellars was established by the late Joe Heitz. Today the winery is managed by Heitz's children, winemaker David and Heitz Wine Cellars president, Kathleen.

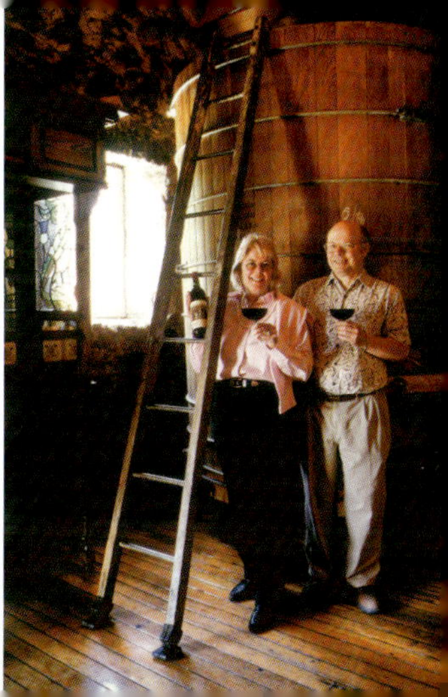

Joseph Phelps Vineyards
Joseph Phelps, a construction engineer, came full circle when he founded Joseph Phelps Vineyards in 1972. Having spent his childhood working on his family's farm, Joseph's new 600-acre ranch located in Spring Valley east of St. Helena reconnected him to his farming roots. The Vineyards' first vintage was a 1973 Johannisberg Riesling, released in 1974.

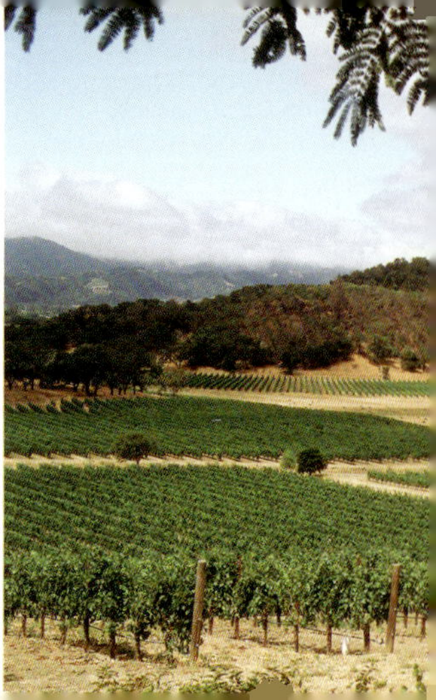

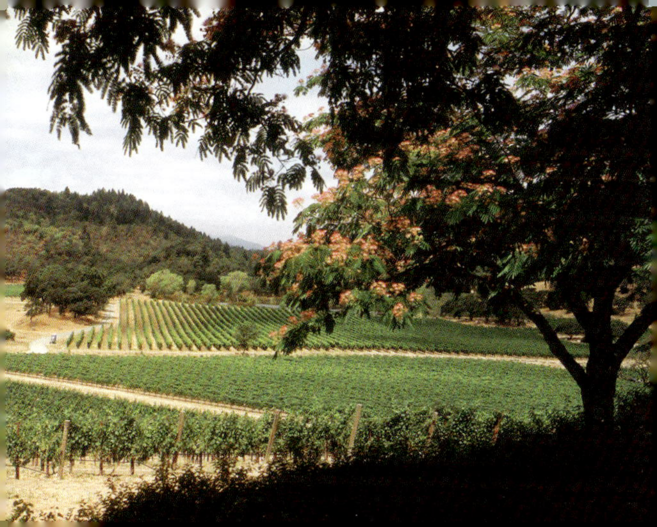

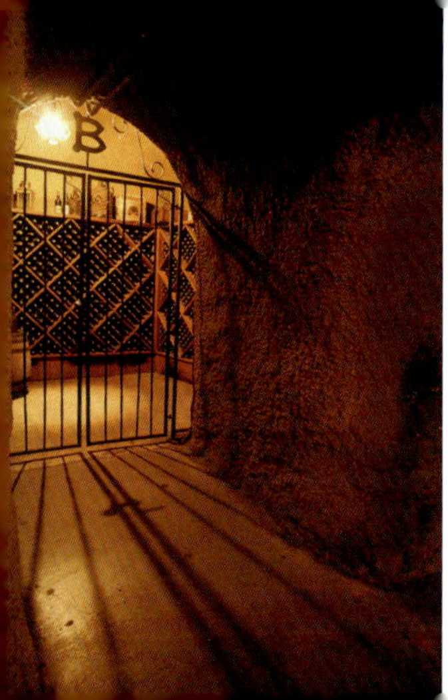

Left One of the oldest Napa Valley wineries, Beringer Vineyards has been producing wines since 1876. Located just north of St. Helena, the winery was established by two German-born brothers, Jacob and Frederick Beringer.

Right High above the St. Helena Highway is St. Clement Vineyards. The winery was built in 1878 for a German immigrant, Fritz Rosenbaum, and his family. Today the estate is owned by Beringer Blass Wine Estates.

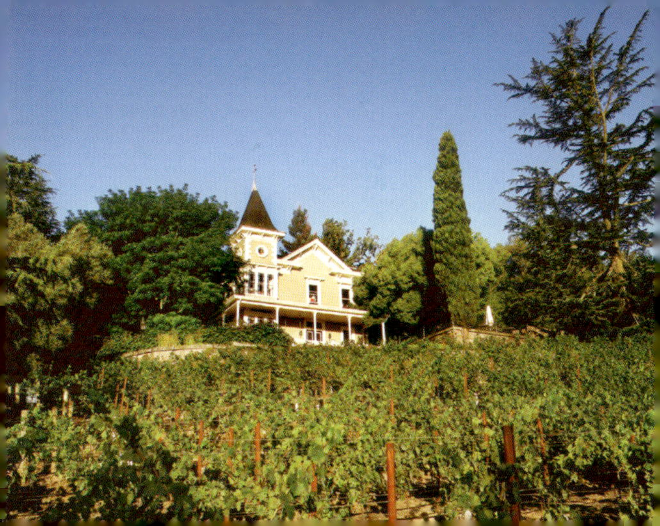

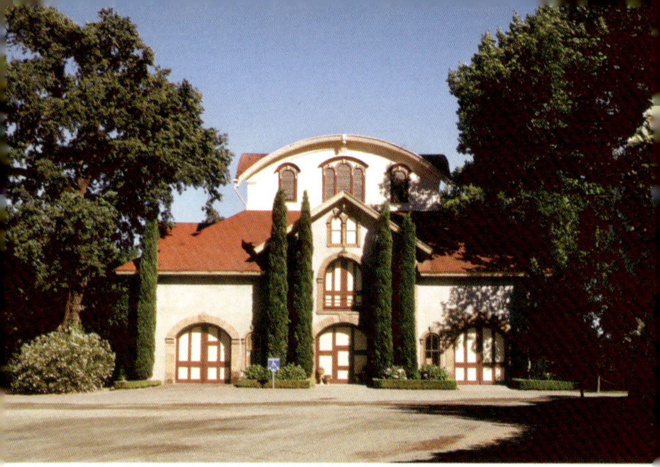

56 Charles Krug Winery is the oldest Napa Valley winery in operation.

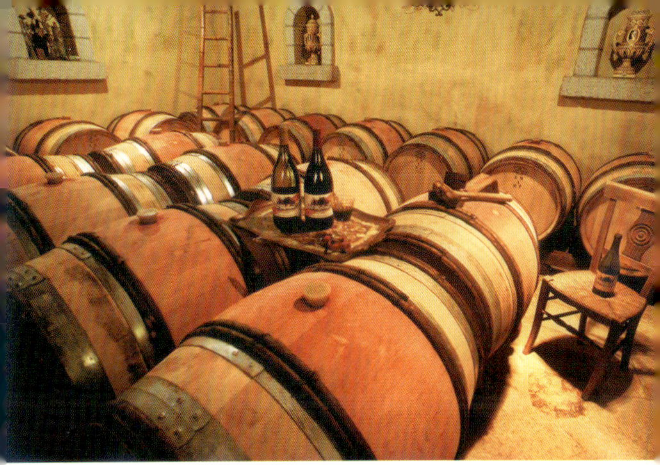

The concrete, stone, and wood winery at El Molino was built in 1871.

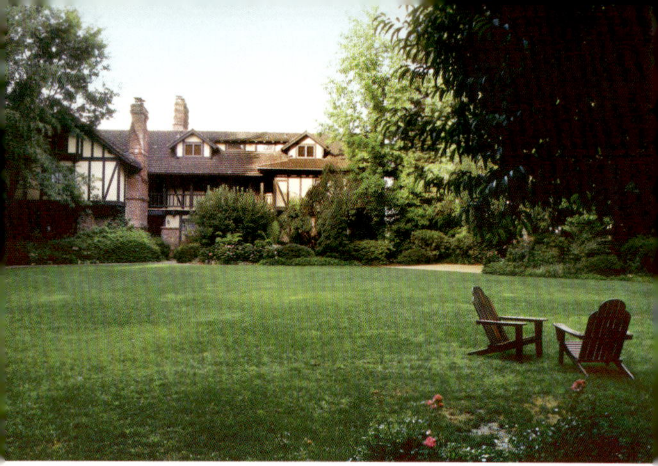

 Old World luxury can be found at Harvest Inn in St. Helena.

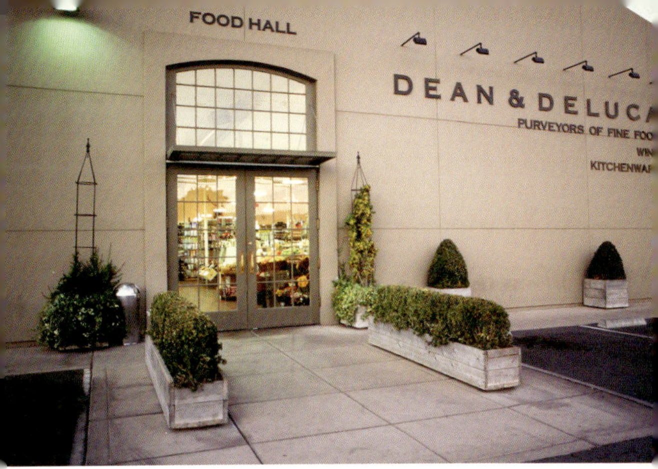

Dean & DeLuca is a favorite stopover for food and wine lovers.

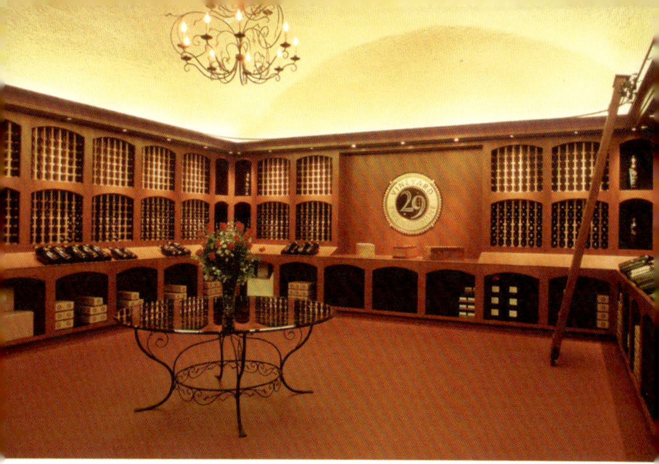

60 At Vineyard 29, tech-savvy and traditional methods are used.

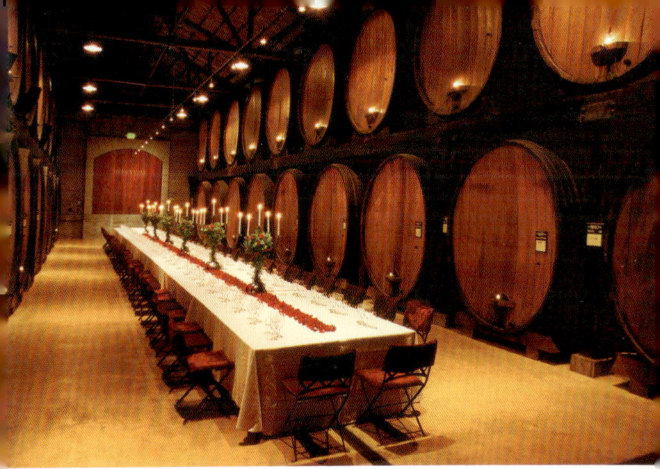

Merryvale's Cask Room is lined with century-old wine barrels.

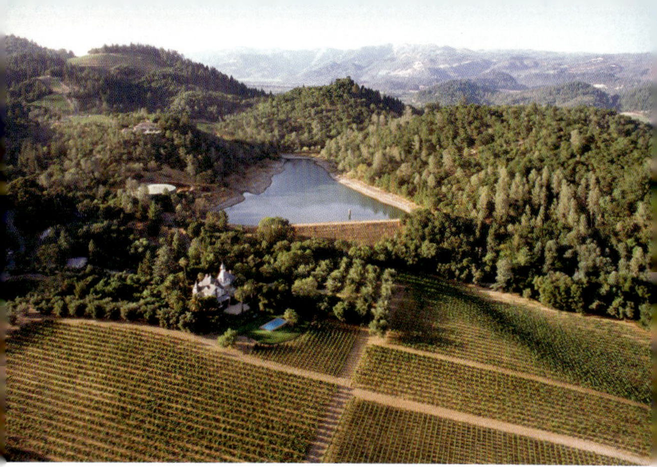

62 Spring Mountain Winery is set amidst hills, west of St. Helena.

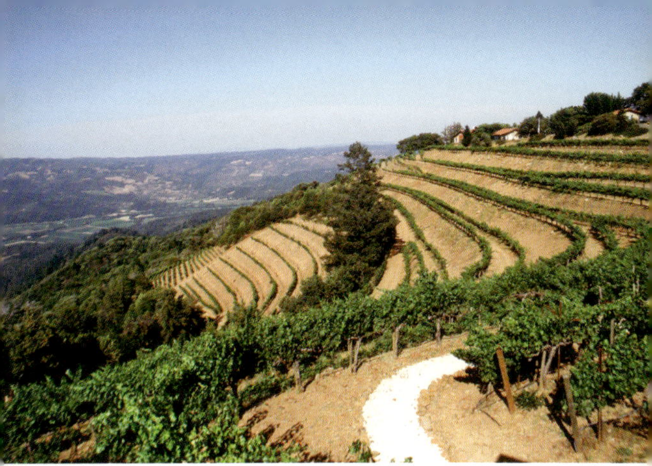

The vineyards at Barnett grow at an elevation of about 2,000 feet.

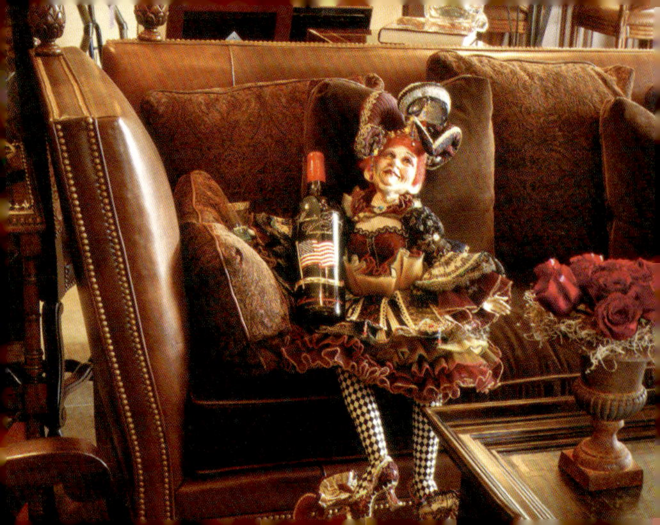

Left Steve and Linda Sherwin purchased their Spring Mountain property in 1996. Since then, Sherwin Family Vineyards has made productive use of its location to craft premium wines.

Right A California State Historical Landmark, Bale Grist Mill was completed in 1846. It provides a rare glimpse into early Napa Valley life.

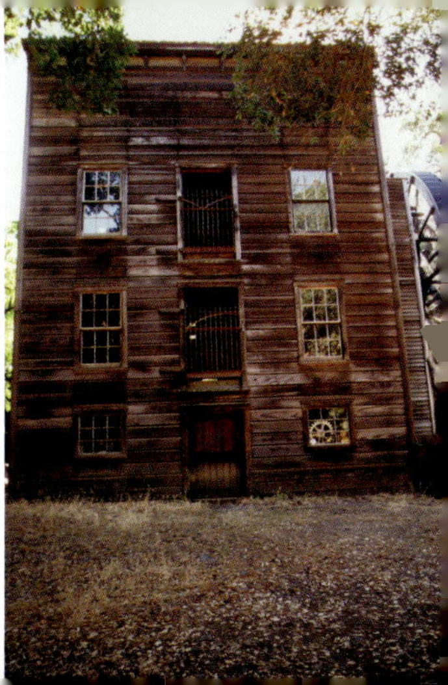

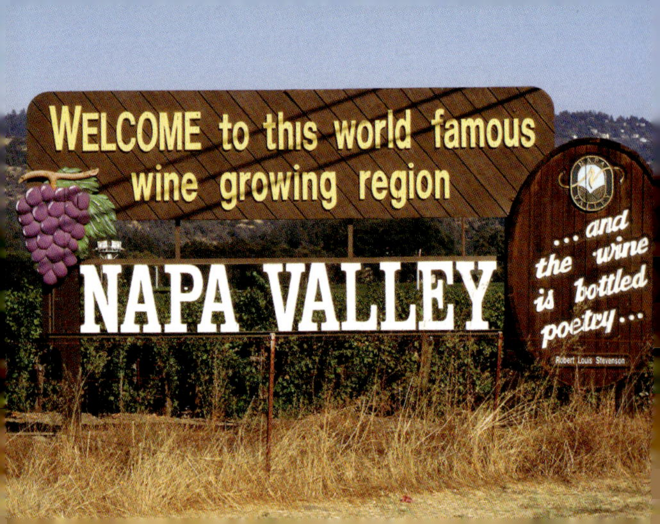
WELCOME to this world famous
wine growing region
NAPA VALLEY
... and the wine is bottled poetry ...
Robert Louis Stevenson

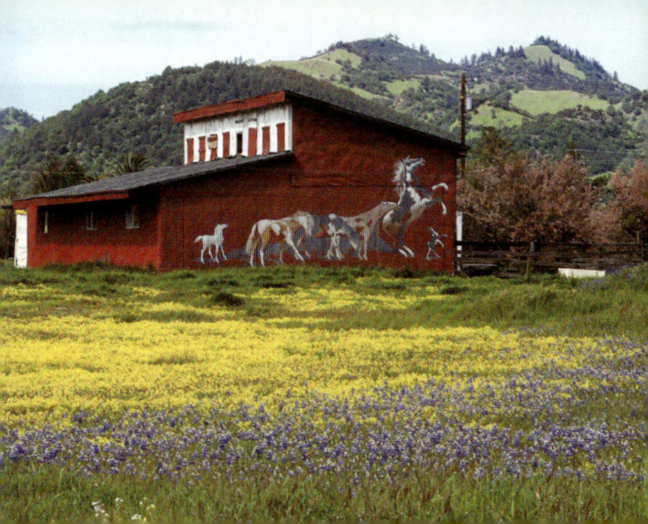

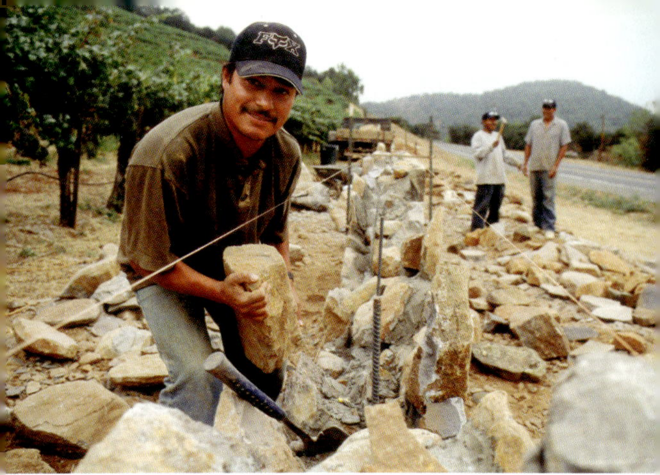

68 Napa County is renowned for its traditional stone walls.

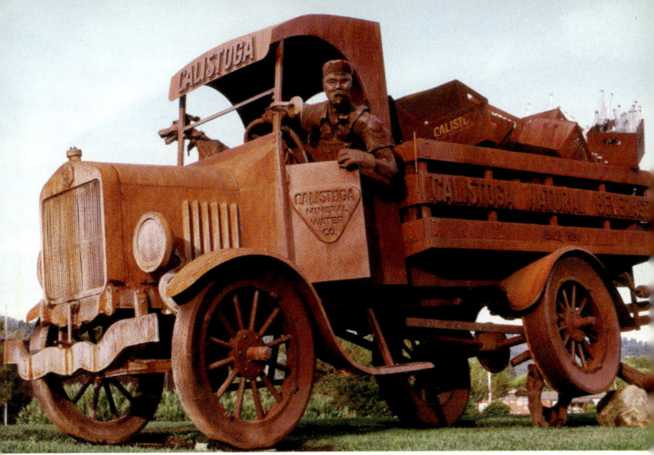

The sculpture, *Guiseppe's Truck*, 'delivers' Calistoga Mineral Water.

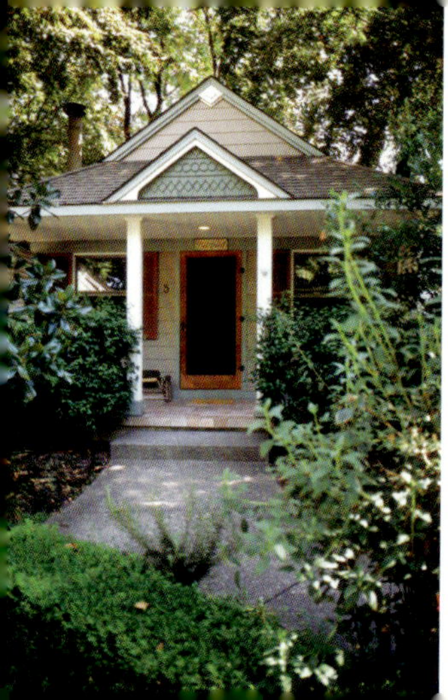

Cottage Grove Inn One of Calistoga's special oases of peace and serenity, Cottage Grove Inn is the fulfillment of a vision created by three friends. Designed to complement the grove of beautiful old Siberian elm trees, each private cottage is a blend of technological conveniences and old style featherbed comfort.

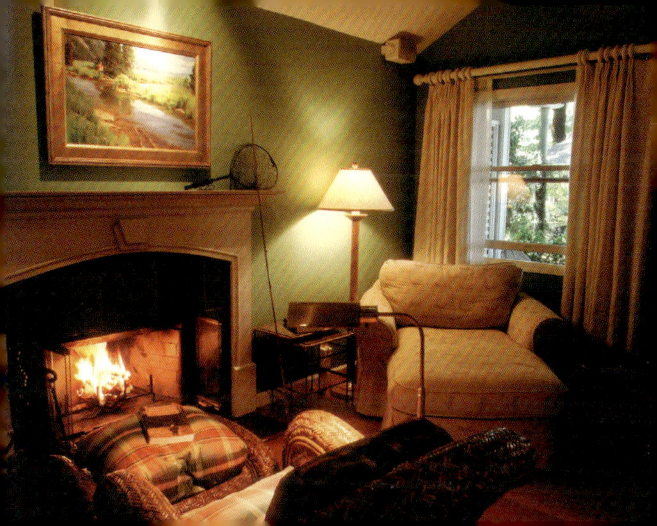

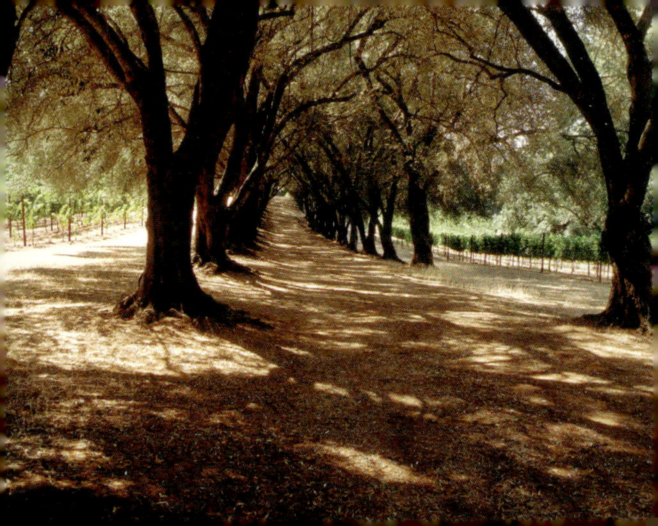

Left Old growth forests are evident throughout Napa Valley, and stands of elm, eucalyptus, and old olive trees can be found tucked away on old properties in the valley.

Right Three palms grace the former estate of famed San Francisco socialite, Lillie Hitchcock Coit. The estate is now home to the Three Palms Vineyard.

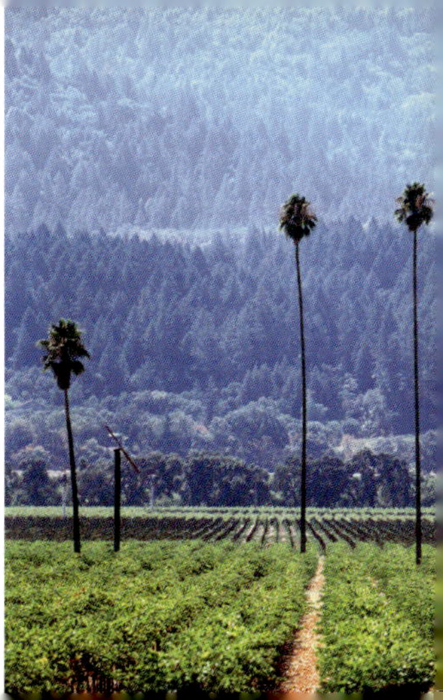

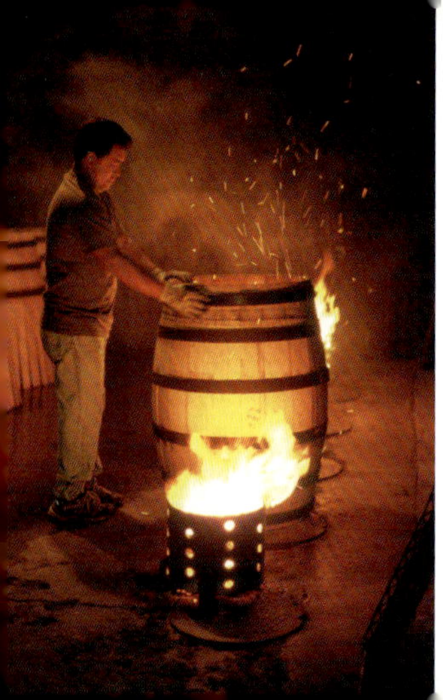

The art of the cooper

The cooper's is an ancient craft. Little has changed with the passing of time; wine barrels are still constructed and bent by hand from the finest oak staves by master coopers who perform their craft with precision and meticulous attention to detail. Barrel-aged red wine takes on a richer hue while barrel-aged white wine gains a golden color.

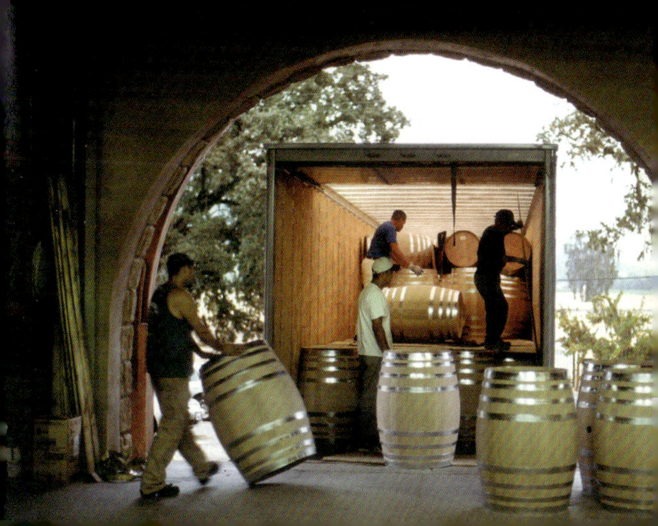

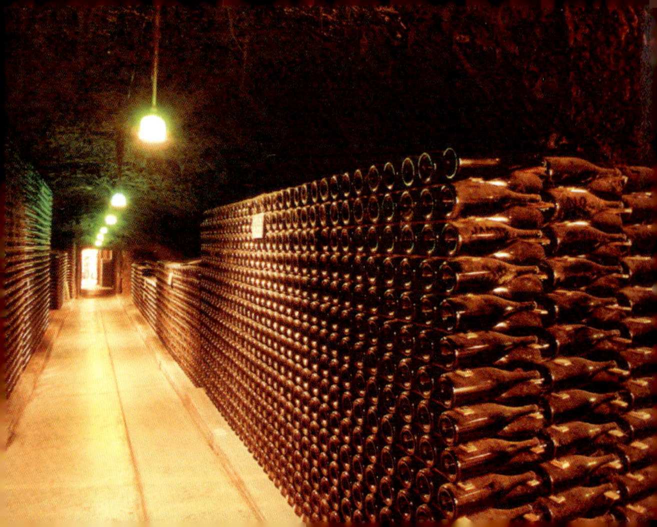

Left Schramsberg was established in 1862 by German immigrants Jacob and Annie Schram. Today, under the stewardship of the Davies family, Schramsberg is renowned for its premier sparkling wines.

Right Many of Napa Valley's estates were originally part of land grants, or *ranchos* in Spanish, given by the Mexican government between 1836 and 1846 to its friends and allies.

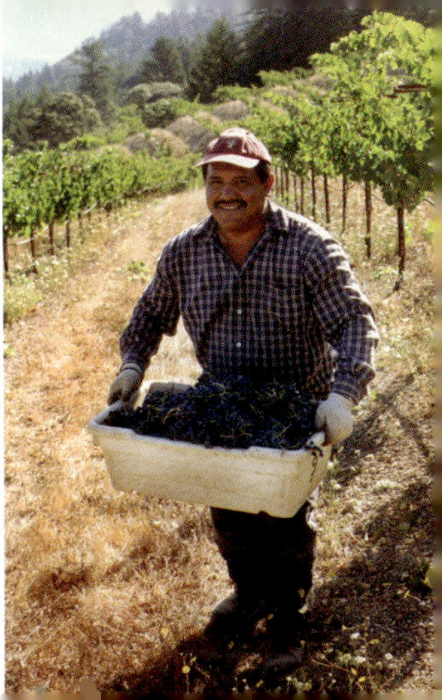

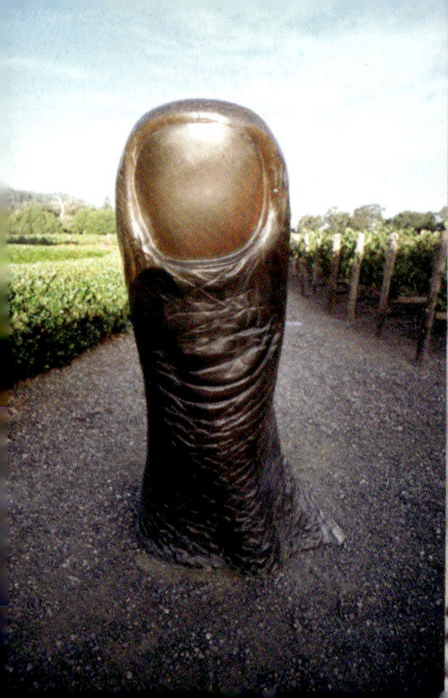

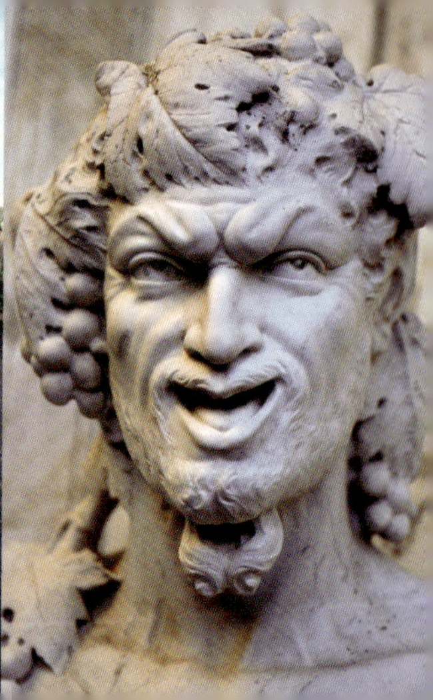

Left Clos Pegase combines architecture, art, and the fine craft of winemaking. Two of the works that can be viewed at Clos Pegase are a six-foot bronze statue of a thumb by Cesar Baldachini (1921–1999) and the *Torino Royal Bacchus* created in the 19th century.

Right Just two miles north of Calistoga is Old Faithful Geyser of California, one of Napa Valley's biggest attractions.

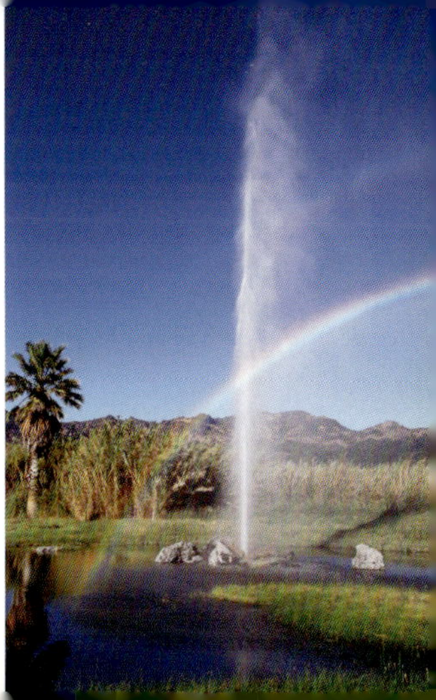

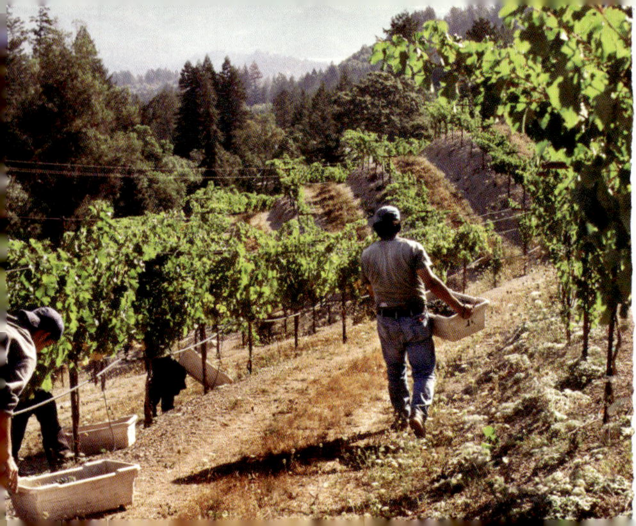

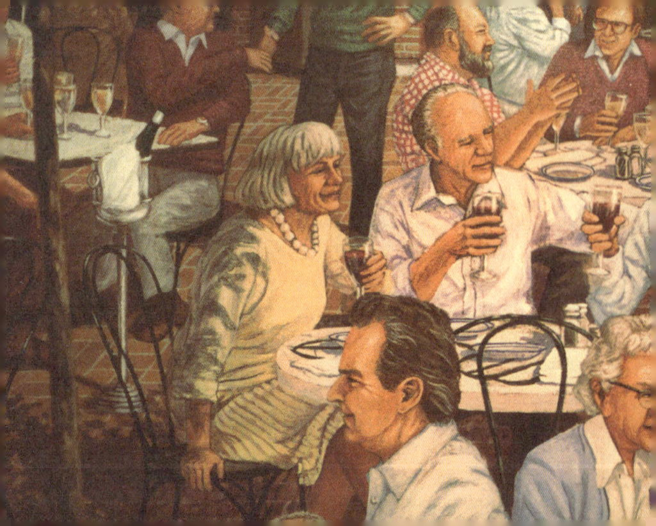